Want Priority Access to FREE eBooks Additional Materials for this Book?

As we release NEW eBooks, we offer them for FREE for a limited time. You will be the FIRST one to know when they are FREE. Join 1000's of insiders who are getting access to FREE Kindle book promotions weekly.

Click HERE for FREE additional material and FREE eBooks- www.rictamilypublishing.com

Table of Contents

Introduction

When you turn on the TV, it is almost impossible that you will not see any advertisement about skin care products. Judging by how much air time that they can afford for these commercials, Skin care product companies must be earning very well just for the small wonder bottles of their bestselling skin care brand. It is no secret that it is a big industry. And why not? Any woman wants an easy fix for their dried and damaged skin. The advertisements promise at least to soften and moisturize the skin, and it shows that it is true judging by the skin of their highly paid models.

The shocking truth is, commercially made soaps and products are all artificial promises. True, they help your skin in one way or the other, but they also do more harm than good to our skin. It is all made from chemicals, some of which are industrially manufactured and are not naturally organic, some are even harmful to our skin if used for a long time.

This eBook will introduce you to a healthier alternative which is the Homemade Soap. Homemade soap is a skin care product that uses natural ingredients that are helpful to our skin. It has long been tested since the beginning of time that herbs and other natural ingredients such as milk and honey provide our body with the protection that it needs, it also has its specific characteristics that provide us specific uses for each such as anti-bacterial properties and natural anti-aging capabilities.

This eBook will give you an idea of the benefits of homemade soap to our body. You will get to know its specific ingredients that make it better that your commercial soaps. We will be taking up the basic process of making the soap and its basic ingredients that make it wonderful to our skin when used. You will now get an idea why it gives that refreshing and relaxing feeling. It is no secret actually, everything is about what you put in the soap that gives its characteristics.

We also added some recipes for soap making that you may try in your own homes. You will soon know and experience how easy it is to make soap. We also threw in different variations of the process so you will get an idea that there are different ways of how to do it.

It is time to break free from your old habit of using those harmful soaps and skin care products. You can go all natural and even go all organic. Start healing your damaged skin and get rid of the accumulated toxins in your body brought about by commercial soap. Turn the page and discover the delightful and new information about the wonders of homemade herbal soap.

Chapter 1
What is a Homemade Herbal Soap?

Homemade soap is a soap made from natural oils and essences. It is a soap in its truest form. Unlike the commercially prepared soap from some big companies, homemade soap does not contain additives that dries up our skin and leaves it damaged. These additives are also the cause of most of the allergies that people get from soap. Homemade soap is made through the process called saponification. In the soap making process, a substance called lye is mixed with fats and oils to produce soap and its by-product glycerine.

History

Some references say that soap making can be traced far back as the Babylonian era. There are reports that excavations of ancient ruins show evidences that people back then uses soap for cleaning. They use fats mixed with other things such as ashes, urine, other oils, to name a few.

Aside from that, herbs, oils, from vegetables and plants and some other substances as milk and honey are used since the beginning of time as a natural treatment for skin diseases. They also make use of these substances in cosmetics and skin care. Cleopatra is probably the most famous believer of bathing in milk and honey is good for the skin. Some people now are still doing that.

It is not a secret that these natural cleansers are already tried and tested. They're cleansing, healing and anti-aging capabilities are proven through time.

Soap By-Product: Glycerin

Glycerin is produced as a by-product of soap. It has a high moisturizing capability. It is sold separately and is almost sold as much as a soap would cost. Glycerin is also used as a special type of soap called glycerin soap. It is used by people with very sensitive skin. Because of glycerin's moisturizing capabilities, it prevents skin from drying up, thus, preventing irritation. It is also one of the main ingredient in the production of some other skin care products like lotion. Some homemade soap leaves the glycerin by-product in the soap, making their finished soap a cleanser as well as a moisturizer.

Addition of Herbs

Herbs and other essential oils are usually added to soap to create a soap which is an answer to a specific need. The herbs on soap actually impart its characteristic to the finished product and therefore creating a special type of soap. These are then called herbal soaps.

Among the most popular herbal soaps out there is Chamomile Soap, Tea Tree Oil Soap, Lavender Soap and Cinnamon Soap. Chamomile Soap promotes relaxing of tired muscles as its most special characteristic. Tea Tree Oil Soap penetrates the skin and relive it of the toxins that has been accumulated there for a long term use of chemical agents. Lavender Soap is probably the most popular because of its scent, but aside from that, lavender is very effective to treat sunburnt skin and skin distress. Cinnamon Soap is a delicious treat for your skin. Not only that it will leave you smelling like Christmas, it is also very effective defoliant which gets rid of old tired skin cells.

Since there are many commercially made soaps that you can easily buy from your local supermarkets you might be asking yourself, why make your own soap. You are probably thinking that it is just basically the same, that using commercially made soap works for you and are already using it for a long time with no problem whatsoever.

The problem here is you do not have any idea what goes in those chemical bars. They are filled with additives that harmful to use for a long period of using. By making your own soap in the comfort of your own homes, you can be sure to have the best ingredients that you can ever wish for in a bar of soap. Aside from its skin care benefits, there are also a lot of other benefits that you can get from making it at home. You will be surprised that this project will be a delight to make and probably continue doing it for a long time.

Best for Sensitive Skin

Whatever your special needs for your skin are, you can get with a special kind of soap that you can easily concoct right at home. However, probably the most notable characteristic of a homemade soap is its ability to cleanse the skin naturally and gently which is perfect for sensitive skin. You can rest assured that there are no products that goes into your soap that could trigger your allergies and make your skin dry or itchy.

Adds to your Savings

Some people would say that some homemade soap is more expensive that the commercially available ones. That is true for some special soaps. However, other commercially prepared, special soap cost a lot too. That is basically why it is better if you make your own soap. The ingredients for making soap is readily available. It does not need special equipment for use for making too. If you make your batch of soap, it would definitely be cheaper than buying one on special stores.

Also, if you are one of those who would like to make use of their extra time being productive, you can earn from this delightful hobby. All of the natural benefits of the soap are there already, it only takes a little creativity to create beautiful soaps that are market-ready. It sells on its own because everybody knows the benefits that they can get from homemade soaps. You don't have to even worry a bit about that.

A Delightful Hobby

If you are a homemaker and you have a lot of time on your hands when the kids are already in school. You can easily pick up a soap making as your hobby. It is always a delight knowing you are spending your time doing something useful and being productive. You may also invite your friends or involve your kids in making the soap. Make project a group project and make use of this time as a bonding moment among yourselves. Also, you will find out that there is already a calming effect while making the soap. This is because some of the essential oils and aroma are released into the air while making it.

Chapter 3
Benefits of Using Herbal Soaps in Adults

We have discussed some of the main benefits of using homemade herbal soaps. We would like to discuss some of the benefits deeper so you can have a better grasp of which ingredients to use when you start making it. Since some of these benefits are very specific and target specific types of needs. We felt that making it into two parts will be better for you to have a better idea. We divided into benefits for adult and for children since they have very different needs.

In this chapter, we take the most important benefits of homemade herbal soaps in adults. You may notice some adult could be very tired from working and it shows in their skin. Some adults may already have aging skin even if their age are not yet in the advance stage. These are brought about by the abuse that our skin is getting from the elements and chemicals that we thought that would help our skin to recover. Sometimes, long-term used of these so-called skin care products does more damage than good. We do so much to our skin when all it needs is a little time-out. Let us find out more how we can care for our skin using homemade herbal soaps and revive it to its natural glow.

Cleanses the Body Gently

As discussed earlier, homemade herbal soaps only have natural ingredients and does not contain additives that are harmful to the skin. Because of this, it gently cleanses the body without washing natural body oils which are needed by the skin, thus, preventing skin dehydration and irritation. It also allows for natural moisturizing keeping the skin soft.

Reduce Skin Aging

Some women would give everything to have a young-looking skin. However, damage from harmful elements makes it difficult for some women to keep their skin from aging. Sensitive skin can easily agitate by dust, continuous exposure to direct sunlight, salt in the air and basically any chemical that we use to our skin thinking it would help us.

Some homemade herbal soap contains ingredients that specifically fight aging. Some example are Aloe Vera Herbal Soap and Carrot Herbal Soap. Aloe Vera has naturally occurring anti-aging properties while carrots has beta-carotene that keeps skin from aging. There are many other kinds of herbal soap that help us with our skin aging woes. We just need to find the right kind for your skin.

Fights Toxins

There is a saying, what touches on your skin goes inside your body. It is actually true, therefore, you need extra care deciding what touches your skin. There are cases that because of long-term use of commercially made soaps, some small amount of toxin gets gathered below the skin surface causing damage. Herbal soaps can help you with that problem.

There are herbal soap with toxin-release capabilities that penetrates your skin, deeply cleansing it and removing harmful substances that gets stuck there. Some of these soaps are partnered with other essential oil to help keep the skin smooth and moisturized while detoxifying it.

Chapter 4
Benefits of Using Herbal Soap to Infants and Young Children

In the previous chapter, we learned about the different benefits of homemade herbal soap in adults. We learned that it helps the skin get the time out from harmful chemical that it needed. We also learned about its anti-aging capabilities. Lastly, we learned how it helps the skin get back its natural glow by removing the toxins accumulated under the skin by long-term use of harmful chemicals.

In this chapter, we will learn about the benefits of herbal soap in infants and young children. We are all aware that a baby's skin is very sensitive because they are just developing antibodies to fight diseases brought about by outside elements. They usually need special soaps that are gentle and does not contain harmful additives and perfumes that may irritate their skin. Because of this, we may consider homemade herbal soap to be the best skin product that we can use gently clean our babies' sensitive skin. Aside from that, here are other basic benefits of homemade soap for children.

Best for Babies

There are different baby soap that is readily available in supermarkets and drugstores. They claim to be very gentle on your child's skin, however, are you willing to bet on that? The thing is, we do not know what goes into making those kinds of soaps. To be sure, it is better to use all natural homemade soap. You can rest assured that only the gentlest ingredients go into making these soaps and it also improves your baby's protection against irritants and other harmful products.

The key to making a guaranteed gentle baby soap is to use high fat formula soap recipe. Also, there are some herbs and ingredients that are best incorporated into baby soaps like olives. Olives are known to antimicrobial properties that keep babies protected while keeping their skin moisturized.

Limit Allergies

Children are prone to allergies because they are just starting to build their natural defenses against harmful agents. If there will be foreign objects in their bodies, it will immediately react to it causing irritation and sometimes infection.

Using homemade herbal soap is best for this because it uses only naturally occurring substances. There are no synthetic materials that may cause allergies and there are no irritants to cause further infection. Furthermore, there are homemade soaps that are 100% organic, meaning there is no way for it to irritate your child's skin as it is all natural.

Protects from Diseases and Infection

Kids are known to easily contract diseases because of their playful nature. They are also prone to get wound injuries which could be infected with bacteria and viruses.

For these you may use homemade herbal soap as a natural remedy. Herbal soap containing turmeric helps cure minor wounds. In addition to that, it is also a very effective cure for skin diseases brought about by fungi like ringworm and athlete's foot. You may also use herbal soap made infused with basil as it helps cure skin irritation, insect bites and even skin acne which is prevalent in young adults.

Chapter 5
Homemade Herbal Soap Better than the Average Supermarket Soap

Our skin is our very first line of defense against the elements; it guards us from direct sunlight, dust from the air and chemicals from different substances. Although it is meant to be blocked harmful elements from our body, it is actually porous in nature. It absorbs and normally stores some toxins in the body. The skin is not equip to get rid of these substances, and their accumulation could lead to a dangerous level and which can also result to sickness. Should you ever get curious and check the ingredients, on these so-considered "great-smelling" and "beautifully packaged" skin care product, you will be surprised to find out that some of them should not even be touching our skin, one of those chemicals formaldehyde which is present in some shampoos.

Using natural herbal soaps will protect our skin from harmful effects of using chemical products that we used over time. It is made from natural oils from plants and some of the special essences that have specific benefit to our skin. It is also incorporated with herbs that helps us fight aging and help our skin to go back into being healthy again.

Oil is naturally found on our skin. Its main purpose is to lock the moisture inside our skin so as not to let our skin dry. What commercially prepared soap does is strip our skin of the natural oils with the chemicals present in them, thus, making our skin dry. On the other hand, homemade herbal soaps do not contain the chemicals that dissolve these oils. In fact, they contain substances that actually lock the moisture in, leaving our skin soft and healthy.

From any perspective, homemade soap is better than commercially prepared soaps. There is always an advantage when we know the things that goes into the things that we use regularly. That way, we are sure that we are getting the best care that we deserve. It is not always good that we only base our judgment from advertisement that we see on the television, knowing first hand that we are using all natural products can make ourselves feel at ease.

Chapter 6
Basic Herbal Soap Making Principle

In the previous chapters we learned what a Homemade Soup means. We also learned about the benefits of homemade herbal soap to our body, that incorporating essential oils and herbs will do wonders to our skin and body as well as to our whole being.

We also learned the advantage of making our own herbal soap at home. We also took up the advantage of using homemade soap over commercially produced soap that are readily available in the supermarket.

Probably, you are by now wondering how you will be able making your own homemade soap. Before we talk about the actual process, we would like to give you a brief background about the soap making principle. This will give you an idea how a soap is made and the process that it undergoes in. It will help you understand and figure out how to make different variety of soap and what you could incorporate in it and which ingredient you may increase or decrease to create the solution that you desire.

The Principle: Saponification

The soap making process uses the Saponification principle. Saponification comes from the Latin origin, which directly translates to "turning into soap or making a soap". In chemistry, it is defined as the chemical process in which oils and fats or their fatty acids react with Lye to produce soap and glycerin. Glycerin is a by-product of soap as we learned in the first chapter.

Although the saponification process is very simple, it is actually a very long process to complete. On the average, a chemical reaction between Oils/Fats and Lye will take about 24 to 48 hours of completion. You can speed the reaction up or slow the reaction down further by controlling the temperature. Which also brings us to the different ways of making soap.

Main Ingredients

Fats and Oils. Oils for soap making comes from vegetable or fruit. Some of the most popular vegetables and fruits that are used for soap making are coconut, avocado, sesame, palm, peanut and a lot more. While fats come from animals, it could be from beef, mutton, lard, etc. Each of these oils and fats have different characteristics and special use. Some are soft and some are hard. Some of these are better cleanser than the others. And some are wonderful skin care products.

Lye. Lye could either be sodium hydroxide or potassium hydroxide. It is a basic compound that is highly soluble in water. It is made from leaching or extracting it from the ashes. Sodium hydroxide and potassium hydroxide, although both referred to as lye are completely different. They are used differently. In soap production, sodium hydroxide is used by making solid or bar soaps while due to its highly soluble characteristics, potassium hydroxide is used mainly in making liquid soap.

Herbal Infusions. Plant and herb extract is added to the soap to give it its distinct characteristic. Whether to make it more beneficial to the skin or to give off soothing effect on muscles, there are simply limitless options for you. You can even make your own recipes depending on your needs.

Chapter 7
Herbal Soap Making Do's and Don'ts

After the last chapter, you should have a little idea by now about the soap making process. However, before we start you with the actual procedure, we would like to give some pointers first. These are guides to follow. These guides should be taken to heart before trying to make your own soap. Remember, you will be dealing with the heat and some corrosive materials in making your soap. You should always remember to take responsibility for your own safety.

Do's

1. Read the instruction on the procedure carefully. If you do not know how to do some of the procedures, you may find some videos on the Internet which may help you better to understand the procedure. Remember, DO NOT START if a step is not clear to you.

2. Have the all protective tools ready before you start heating things up. Have your goggles to protect your eyes and gloves to protect your skin from burns. Choose a working area near where there is a running water for when you get burnt or something gets in your eyes.

3. Measure everything accurately. Beginner soap makers always tend to forget to follow this reminder. You should take special care measuring everything because some reactions will not take place or worse, if some of the ingredients are added in huge amount, a rapid reaction may occur and may cause accidents. This is most important when making your lye solution.

4. Have all the ingredients ready, you do not want to stop at halfway just because you forgot to prepare one of the ingredients. Some ingredients will not be good to be stored again when chemical reaction already took place. You will be wasting your time and your money if you fail to follow this one simple rule.

5. Enjoy what you are doing. Remember, you are making something wonderful. Smile, relax and marvel at your work.

Don'ts

1. Do not skip a step. Do not feel like a pro and think that you have mastered all the steps already. Keep yourself in check and follow directions earnestly.
2. Do not use materials that can be corroded by Lye. Lye is highly corrosive on its own, it will ruin your Teflon, aluminium, tin and iron kitchen wares. It is better if you could find some bowls that will be used and re-used especially for this project alone.
3. Do not do something else while making your soap. Focus is the key here. You want to avoid accidents that should not have happened in the first place if you have just taken the proper care in what you are doing.
4. Do not work in an area where there is no proper ventilation. You should at least have your window or exhaust open when working inside your house. The chemical reaction may produce fumes that is not good when inhaled.
5. Do not worry too much about the outcome. If you are just a beginner soap maker, it is okay to make mistakes at first. It is how you learn. Try again until you get the correct outcome. You can also experiment on adding many different herbs to know what suits your fancy or what you feel is appropriate to your need.

Chapter 8
Types of Soap Making Methods

As we learned in Chapter 6. There is only one main process of making a soap that is the chemical process of saponification. While the principle remains the same, there are still other types of soap making process. They only differ in terms of the methods use, but they are essentially the same.

Different methods of making soap also produce different types of soaps. There is your regular bar soap, the transparent bar soap, liquid soap, etc. Although they are essentially the same as mentioned, each of these types gives off different experience when used. It is good to try all or most of the methods for you to know which is more comfortable for you to do.

Cold Process

The cold process method is basically the most widely used method among those who make soap from the basic ingredients which is oil or fat and lye. It got the name cold process because heat is not used to speed up reactions or heat anything in this method. A cold bath (iced water) is actually used to lower the temperature of lye that reacted with water as it tend to heat up from the reaction.

Hot Process

The procedure and the idea behind this method is basically the same with the cold method. However, heat is used to speed up the process. It is relatively faster than doing the cold process method and the texture of the soap produce is much more smooth than the once produced in the cold process.

Melt Method

Melt method is used by soap makers who want to skip on the saponification process. What they do is purchase a ready-made soap base, usually a glycerin soap, melt it and infuse it with herbs or plant essence or add whatever materials they fancy.

It is widely used in homes a mother-daughter project as it already skipped in the saponification process which gives off fumes that is not very ideal for kids. Melted soap can easily be poured into molds and wait to dry. Although transparent soaps can be produced by using the hot process. The melt method is the source of most of the transparent soaps that you see in the market.

Re-Batching Method

This method is almost the same with the melt method, only in re-batching you are not using a ready-made soap base. You use your own soap created by the cold process or the hot process, usually the slivers or soap shavings are used here so as not to waste it. You can also use unsuccessful batches in this method. You just gather all of those extra soap in kettle, heat it, when it melts, again, you can add whatever you fancy adding, and pouring it into molds.

Chapter 9
Homemade Herbal Soap Recipes

Finally, here are some recipes that you may try to do at home. There is one sample of each method in this guide. You may also find other free soap making recipes on the Internet. In the meantime, here are the most basic recipes for each kind of method.

Cold Method

Ingredients:

- 142g Sodium Hydroxide (Lye)
- 380ml Distilled Water
- 300g Coconut Oil
- 500g Olive Oil
- 200g Vegetable Shortening/ Palm Oil

Procedure:

1. Make sure to have a spacious, well-ventilated space for working. Wear your protective instruments such as gloves and goggles.
2. Line your molds with parchment paper. Measure out all ingredients carefully. ACCURACY is important. Use heat-proof glass for the water. Heat will be generated as you pour the lye into the water.
3. Prepare your cold water bath. Carefully pour the lye pellets into the water while stirring. It will create heat and fumes. Be careful not to burn yourself or inhale the fumes. Place it in the water bath to speed up lowering down the temperature.
4. While waiting for the lye-water solution to cool down, prepare your oils. If you have solid oils, heat them in a double boiler until melted. Bring the temperature down until same with the lye solution.

5. Pour the lye solution to your oil and carefully stir until you see a trace. You will know that there is a trace when while dipping your spoon and bringing it back up, there is a line that is made (presumed to be soap) that stays a second or two before dissolving back into the mixture. (You may add your herbs and essences when you see the first trace)

6. Continue stirring until there is a hard trace, if done manually, this step may take hours. By this time, your mixture will look like a custard.

7. Pour the mixture into your pre-lined molds. Cover the molds with a towel right away. Leave it for 24 to 48 hours to complete the saponification process.

8. You may take the soap out of the mold and continue air-drying it in another 4-6 weeks depending on how hard you want your soap to be.

Hot Method

For the hot process procedure. Simply follow the cold process recipe only, you may use a crock pot or a pot over a stove to heat your oil-lye mixture in while stirring to speed up the process.

Take Note: This recipe is for basic unscented soap. You may use your mineral oils, herbs, colorant, etc. when you see the first light trace.

Melt Method

Ingredients:

- 1lb Ready-Made Soap Base
- Natural Additives
- Colorant (optional)
- Rubbing Alcohol (optional)

Procedure:

1. Prepare your molds, line them with parchment paper or use silicone molds if available.

2. Cut your ready-made soap base into 1 inch cube or thinner to make melting faster. Place the soap base cubes into a heat proof, microwave safe glass if you want to use a microwave for melting or use a double boiler if you are using the stove.

3. When using the microwave: Set your temperature on high and set the timer to 1 minute. You can easily stir un-melted soap base if there are any. When using the stove top double broiler: melt the soap base until no more solid soap base are left.

4. Add the natural additives of your choice. You may also use essential oils to give your soap fragrance. Just be careful not to overdo it or else you will have a very overpowering scent.

5. Colorants are added while the soap base is still being melted. Add the colorant little by little to achieve the desired color.

6. Pour your mixture into your mold. One good tip is to spray the surface of your soap with rubbing alcohol to eliminate bubbles that would form from heating or adding the colorant. Leave the mold undisturbed until it is hard, usually after a few hours.

Conclusion

Homemade herbal soap is a natural cleansing agent in its truest form. Soap use has been traced thousands of years ago. Its curing and cleansing capabilities have been proven ever during those times. Adding natural occurring oils and essences to your soap could turn it into a special kind of soap which aids in many ways like fighting toxins and infections as well as limiting allergy-causing agents.

Homemade herbal soap is very gentle. It does not rip the body of its natural oils and it does not contain harmful chemicals that can be found in commercially prepared soaps. Instead, it naturally exfoliates our skin, helping it in the anti-aging process. It is also very safe for children and infant's use. It aids in skin revival and it has a holistic effect to the body, adding natural oils and herbs that soothes our mind and our muscles.

There are a lot more benefits that we could get from homemade herbal soap. Aside from its health and skin care benefits, making soap could be a profitable venture. It can also be a very pleasurable hobby for those who has too much time on their hands. It could also be a good group bonding among friends or families.

It is very easy to make soap, however, you have to take care in following instructions. You also have to handle the materials used in soap making with caution. It is always better to be safe than sorry, so, always remember to keep your protective gears handy. Follow all the guidelines well and you will be good to go.

When making soap, always remember to enjoy the moment. After all, you are doing something that is supposed to make you feel better. Relax, be creative and have fun.

Review Link

If you enjoyed this book, we would really appreciate it if you could leave us a positive REVIEW?

P.S. You can <u>CLICK HERE</u> to go directly to the book page and leave your review and/or purchase our other books above. Alternatively, you can copy and paste this address into your browser --- http://amzn.to/1wCj3OE

Start with a Bit of Planning

In this chapter you'll learn about how to start planning for the big day. Without proper planning, it is almost impossible to make a long lasting impact. Just read on and discover some cool ways to start the planning process.

Guests are important, we know, but it is the couple that is getting married and should have the most say in the arrangements and settings. The best way to do this is to sit down with your partner, and brainstorm the ideas. Think about what fascinates you the most a ballroom dinner, mountaintop ceremony or a beach bash. Remember, that you are not finalized anything here, you are just brainstorming the ideas and some of them are likely to be very childish, unrealistic and impractical. No matter what, just stick to your wishes and do not think about the money yet.

Here it is also a good idea to decide the date of the event, a tentative one would do. If you are not sure about the date you may need to discuss it with other family members. Deciding the season or the month would make things easier for the rest of the planning. Deciding about the date, month or season becomes essentially more important if your plan involves travelling.

Cover All Aspect

Determine the size of your event; this can help you have the rough cost estimation likely to be incurred on your wedding. You obviously don't want to forget anyone, so making a guest list should be the most important part of your planning. Don't try to make this list in a single go but do it slowly so that you don't forget anyone. Although you are not really planning in terms of money here but you should always remember that price usually goes up per guest. In case you're planning includes travelling, make sure you create a separate plan for that. This includes things like advance ticket booking and choosing the right accommodation.

Money Talk

Let's talk money now. It is rare for parents bear the full monetary burden of their children's marriage (Considering the current economic environment, they are not to be blamed either). Having an idea of how many parents from both sides would be contributing is really helpful. If it is a hefty amount, you are lucky - if not, then you should continue reading to make your marriage stand out on a tight budget.

It is time to organize your planning. Get a notebook and start writing down your estimated budget (separated into different categories like dresses, decorations etc.) This will help you compare the actual spending with what you have estimated. In case you have spent a little more than anticipated in a particular category, you can always look for ways to bring down the cost in some other category – this will keep things even.

This is what Anna Burrel, famous American Chef has to say about planning and organizing.

"Organizing ahead of time makes the work more enjoyable. Chefs cut up the onions and have the ingredients lined up ahead of time and have them ready to go. When everything is organized you can clean as you go, and it makes everything so much easier and fun"

It wasn't that difficult, was it? Moving on to the next chapter you'll learn some simple tips and suggestions on how you can find that perfect venue and more.

If you like this preview, then *click here for the full story of this eBook!*

Or go to: *http://www.amazon.com/dp/B00WGQUTZM/*

Check Out My Other Books

The Top Ten Best Pets for Children
Tips on Care and Proper Choice for your Child

25 Funeral Planning Essentials
The Ultimate Guide for Selecting Funeral Homes, Obituaries and Funeral Directors

Stop Self-Sabotaging and Shift your Paradigm to Success
Your Ultimate Guide to Start Living the Life You Always Wanted

Stop the Negative Self-Talk Today
Quotes and Secrets to Thinking Positively that Will Heal your Soul

Anger, Stress and Fear
Your Personal Guide in Controlling Anger, Managing Stress and Overcoming Fear

Chakras for Beginners
The Ultimate Guide to Balancing Chakras, Radiating Positive Energies and Strengthening Auras

Books of author Elijah Hunter

Productivity Power
Your Daily Guide to Habit Stacking, Preventing Procrastination and Forming Successful Skills

Ultimate Guide to Financial Freedom
Achieve Wealth, Attain Success and Manage your Debt Like the Rich!

Books of author Ricky King

The Nature of True of Intelligence
Musings on theYourient Sumerian Culture from a Christian Perspective

Jesus, Jews & Jerusalem
Past, Present and Future of the City of God

10 Steps against Pornography
A Step Journey to Overcoming Internet Sexual Addiction through Jesus

Gilgamesh: King in Quest of Immortality
An Extra-Biblical Proof for the Genesis Flood

Israel vs the World
The Apple of God's Eye in the End Times

Dedication

To our three blessings that have made RicTamily complete and continue to grow together in His loving embrace.

Disclaimer

The information in this book is in no way intended as medical advice. This book is not meant to be used, nor should it be used, to diagnose or treat any medical condition. The author disclaims responsibility for any adverse health effects that come in combination with the use of methods and suggestions presented in the book. The publisher and author are not responsible for any health or allergy needs that may require medical supervision and are not liable for any damages or negative consequences from any treatment, action, application or preparation, to any person reading or following the information in this book.

Made in the USA
Lexington, KY
18 September 2016